DRAGONS
AND OTHER LEGENDARY CREATURES

L. J. TRACOSAS

W9-BCN-030

becker&mayer!

CONTENTS

THAR BE DRAGONS . . . EVERYWHERE!

Welcome to the world of dragons! In this book, you'll learn everything you need to know about these fierce legendary beasts. You'll explore information about one of the most popular dragons in the world: the European dragon. These mythic creatures terrorized villages and hoarded gold, battled knights, and breathed fire.

But there's a whole world full of dragons, and you can read about many of them here. Dragon lore can be found all over the world—from the frozen landscapes of Scandinavia to the deserts of Africa to the waterways of Southeast Asia. Some of these dragons are kind, some are evil. Some fly and shoot flames from their mouths, some love to help people. But all of them are fantastic!

Along the way, you'll read about dragon mythology and what might have inspired these stories, see how dragons show up in history and culture throughout the centuries, plus learn about modern-day dragons—real-life creatures that still carry the dragon name.

HERE BE DRAGONS

Where does your favorite dragon come from?

AMPHIPTERE
EUROPE

KNUCKER
BRITAIN

EUROPEAN DRAGON
WESTERN EUROPE

WYVERN
EUROPE

SVARA
EASTERN EUROPE

ZILANT
RUSSIA

Y DDRAIG GOCH
BRITAIN

ZMEY GORNYNYCH
EASTERN EUROPE/RUSSIA

IMUGI
ASIA

GARGOUILLE
NORTHEASTERN FRANCE

HYDRA
MEDITERRANEAN

CHIMERA
SOUTHEASTERN EUROPE

LONG
CHINA

AMARU
PERU

TARASQUE
SOUTHERN EUROPE

ETHIOPIAN DRAGON
EASTERN AFRICA

PAKHANGBA
INDIA

NĀGA
SOUTHEASTERN ASIA

COCKATRICE
NORTHERN AFRICA

CREATURE FEATURES

What do dragons look like? There's a lot of variety in the dragon world! While many dragons have unique characteristics, here are a few that many—but not all—dragons share.

Ssssnake-like body

The word dragon comes from the Greek and Latin words for "serpent." Nearly every dragon in these pages has a serpent's body or tail.

Leathery wings

Not every dragon has wings—and even those that do have wings don't necessarily fly. Many dragons have batlike wings made up of extended bones with a leathery skin-flap forming the wing.

Terrible teeth

All dragons have gaping jaws filled with sharp teeth. Some carry precious stones in their mouths, and others just have teeth the length of your arm.

Horrible Horns

Most dragon species have multiple horns, which are used for display to threaten and ward off enemies, and are also used in battle.

Exceptional Eggs

Dragons have been known to lay anywhere from one to five eggs in what's called a "clutch," and a dragon may lay several clutches during its lifetime.

Mighty Tails

If you manage to get past a dragon's cunning wit, fiery breath, horrible horns, and powerful claws, its terrifying tail might be just the thing to whip around and destroy an enemy with its massive force. A dragon's tail can be tipped with either a club, spikes, barbs, thorns, or even fire!

Weaponlike Claws

Depending on the type of dragon, it may have anywhere from three to five toes equipped with deadly claws sharp enough to clutch enemies and prey from the sky, and then shred it to pieces. Some dragons have retractable claws.

Indestructible Scales

A dragon's body is covered with scales, which are soft when they're born and grow to become extremely dense and hard that overlap and act as its armor, protecting its sensitive body. The scales can withstand high impact, such as a direct sword-blow.

THE DRAGON OF ALL DRAGONS

As you'll see in this book, not all dragons are evil monsters. In many Eastern cultures—Asia and India, for example—dragons are kind creatures that bring wealth, plentiful crops, and water. Some also protect important people and places. But we'll get to these dragons later.

A BAD RAP

Many dragons in Western culture—mostly those from Europe—have bad reputations. At the very least, they cause mischief; at their worst they are responsible for death and destruction.

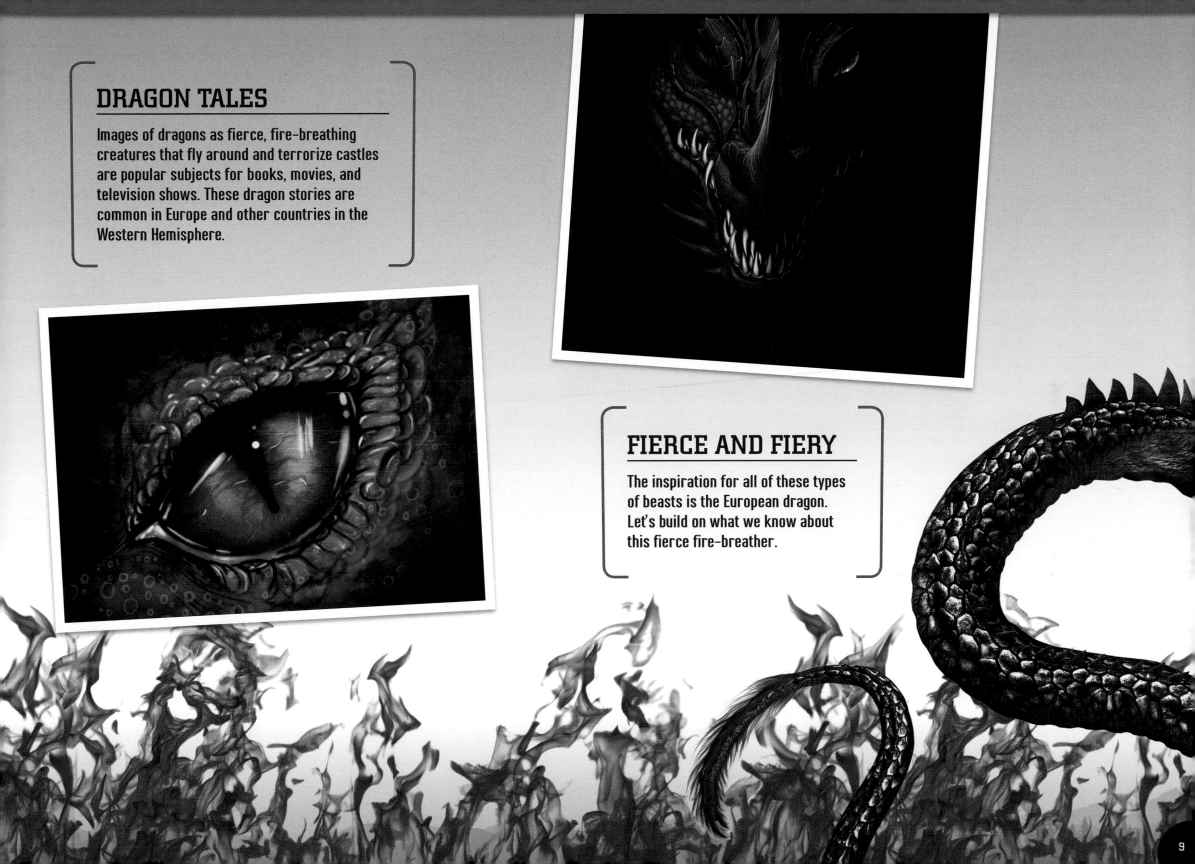

DRAGON TALES

Images of dragons as fierce, fire-breathing creatures that fly around and terrorize castles are popular subjects for books, movies, and television shows. These dragon stories are common in Europe and other countries in the Western Hemisphere.

FIERCE AND FIERY

The inspiration for all of these types of beasts is the European dragon. Let's build on what we know about this fierce fire-breather.

EUROPEAN DRAGON

KNIGHT TERROR

According to legend, European dragons could be found in mountain ranges from England to Germany about a thousand years ago. They had huge, scaly bodies, and they could breathe fire. Often, they hoarded piles of gold. These beasts are the real stars of the stories about knights rescuing princesses.

European dragons were carnivores, meaning they ate meat. They had strong teeth with jaws stretching wide enough that they could snap up goats, sheep, and even cows. Sometimes in dragon lore, European dragons even ate people. *Gulp!*

Creature Features

Region	Western Europe
Time Period	5th—15th centuries
Habitat	Mountain caves
Flight Capable	Yes
Fire Breath	Yes

GOOD OR EVIL?

Many tales of the European dragon center around a fire-breathing terror. But are all dragons from Europe mean-spirited monsters? No. In fact, in some ancient Greek and Roman myths, *drakontes*—what they called dragons—are wise and help creatures.

READY FOR TAKEOFF!

European dragons circle in the air and strike like snakes in the sky. They fly with huge wings. However, their wings are more like a bat's than a bird's.

Bat Wing

Bird Wing

BIRD WINGS VS. DRAGON WINGS

Flying creatures in our world can take to the sky—thanks to their wings. But not all wings are alike. A bird's wings are like human arm bones, but with flight-ready feathers that fan out to catch the air. The bones that make up the structure of a bat's wings look more like fingers, over which skin stretches out to catch the air. A dragon's wings resemble the bat's wing, and a dragon's lizardlike skin is stretched over these bones.

Birds and bats both flap their wings by using to the power of their strong chest muscles. Huge, muscular dragons would likely have the same strength to move their wings.

FIGHT WITH FIRE

What's more terrifying than a huge airborne predator? One that breathes fire too. Dragon myths don't try to explain exactly how these beasts could spew flames. But it might have something to do with the many accounts of dragons having poisonous breath. Some stories say that dragons stank of sulfur, an element that can combine with other elements to give off a reeking rotten-egg smell. Sulfur can also be flammable, creating an eerie blue-white flame. Maybe dragons exhaled sulfur in a gas form, which could ignite under the right conditions.

SLAYING THE DRAGON

THE LEGEND OF ST. GEORGE

Perhaps one of the most famous stories that feature the European dragon is the legend of St. George, the dragon slayer. In the story, a terrible dragon terrorizes a town. It has poisoned all the drinking water in the nearby lake, and the people are suffering from thirst. The dragon eats up all the townspeople's sheep and cattle, and then sets its sights on the people themselves. To prevent the dragon from destroying the entire town right away, the town's leader decides that one person a day must be sacrificed to the dragon as a meal.

St. George hears this story and travels to the town. He rides out to the lake where the dragon lives, and he's set on battling the huge beast. The dragon hears him coming and lets out a booming roar. On his horse, St. George gallops up to the creature, with his lance ready to strike. But as the tip collides with the dragon's scales, the lance snaps apart. The dragon's thick scales are like armor, protecting it from being wounded. St. George is knocked off of his horse, but he gets back up. The hero is determined to beat the beast. Suddenly, he notices something. Where the mighty dragon's wing connects to its body, there are no scales— St. George can see the dragon's smooth, serpent skin. He takes out his sword, and with all of his energy, he leaps and strikes the dragon, sinking his sword into this soft spot. St. George slays the dragon.

KNIGHTLY HEROES

During the Middle Ages, which lasted from about the years 1100 to 1450, dragon stories gained popularity—and so did the heroes of these stories: knights. Knights were really soldiers who fought for a lord or a king. To be a knight, young men first became pages, where they would work for noblemen. Then they became squires, where they learned to fight while also helping a knight with his armor and other tasks. Finally, if he did a good job, the young man could become a knight and fight in battle.

THE REAL ST. GEORGE

Though the epic story of St. George slaying the dragon is fiction, St. George was a real person. He was born in Turkey and lived during the third century, sometime around 250 AD. Not much is known about him, although scholars believe he was a soldier and helped spread the ideas of Christianity. Stories about St. George became popular hundreds of years after he died. Today, St. George is the patron saint of England, and he is celebrated on St. George's Day, which is April 23.

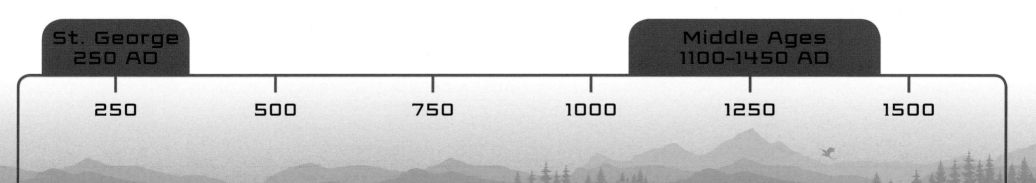

St. George
250 AD

Middle Ages
1100–1450 AD

250   500   750   1000   1250   1500

OTHER DRAGONS FROM EUROPE

While the European dragon is the most popular dragon type in Western lore, other dragons are well-known in different regions of Europe, and each has its own characteristics and stories. Let's explore a few of the other dragons from European mythology.

FRENCH DRAGON

GARGOUILLE

BEWARE THE WATER

Gargouille terrorized fishermen along the river Seine in France. Gargouille had a beaklike jaw filled with jagged upper and lower teeth that fit together almost like a zipper. This huge dragon could whip up waterspouts using its four legs and four wings. It would flip over fishing boats and gobble up their crews. Legend has it that a priest was able to finally stop Gargouille's terror simply by making the sign of the cross.

Creature Features

Region	Europe (Northeastern France)
Time Period	12th century or earlier
Habitat	Waterways, like rivers and lakes
Flight Capable	Yes
Fire Breath	Yes

BUILDING WITH GARGOYLES

Some say Gargouille was the inspiration for gargoyles, the sculpted spouts that spit rainwater away from cathedrals.

ZMEY GORNYNYCH

ONE, TWO, THREE HEADS

Zmey Gornynych, also known as Zmei Gorynich, was a scary sight. It had three snapping, snarling heads, and was as vicious as could be. It was able to walk upright on its strong back legs. Some legends even describe it as being half human and half serpent.

Zmey Gornynych had magical powers, which it used to create chaos and to kidnap people. Because it had three heads, it had three times the teeth of other dragons. Each of its three jaws had a set of two long fangs.

Creature Features

Region	Eastern Europe, Russia
Time Period	Unknown
Habitat	Castles filled with riches
Flight Capable	Yes
Fire Breath	Yes

BAD NEWS

In Western mythology, dragons are often portrayed as wicked and mean. Evil dragons in European legends do all sorts of terrible things, including poisoning water, killing crops, stealing livestock, bringing disastrous storms, piling up and guarding gold, cursing towns, and even eating people.

Y DDRAIG GOCH

THE RED DRAGON

According to Welsh legend, a king was attempting to build a new castle on a hill, but every night an earthquake toppled any construction done that day. Two dragons were trapped underground battling each other and shaking the earth. The eventual victor was Y Ddraig Goch, the red Welsh dragon.

Creature Features

Region	Britain
Time Period	Early 9th century
Habitat	Underground caves
Flight Capable	Yes
Fire Breath	Yes

LEADING THE WAY

Today, Y Ddraig Goch is the symbol of Wales and their motto is "The Red Dragon will lead the way."

AMPHIPTERE

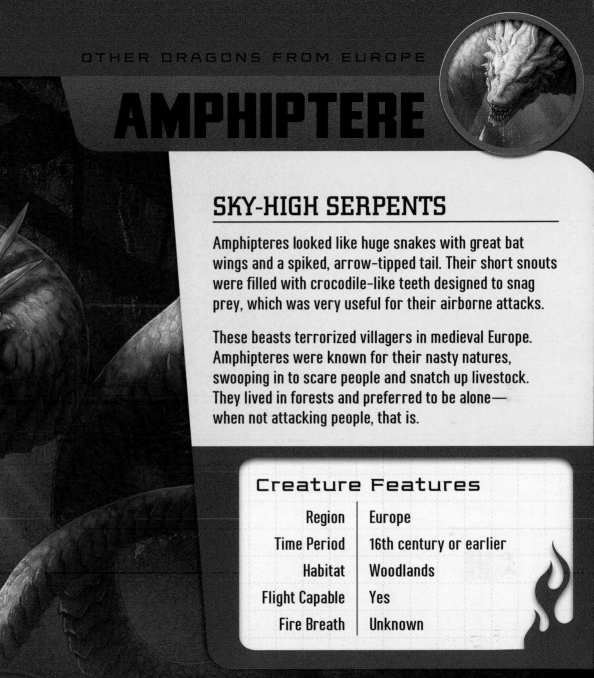

SKY-HIGH SERPENTS

Amphipteres looked like huge snakes with great bat wings and a spiked, arrow-tipped tail. Their short snouts were filled with crocodile-like teeth designed to snag prey, which was very useful for their airborne attacks.

These beasts terrorized villagers in medieval Europe. Amphipteres were known for their nasty natures, swooping in to scare people and snatch up livestock. They lived in forests and preferred to be alone—when not attacking people, that is.

Creature Features

Region	Europe
Time Period	16th century or earlier
Habitat	Woodlands
Flight Capable	Yes
Fire Breath	Unknown

WATERY REALMS

Dragons from all over the world love water. From St. George's dragon, who lived by a lake; to the ancient Greek Hydra, who lived by Lake Lerna; to the lucky Long in China; to the Knucker in its knuckerhole, H2O is almost always in a dragon's habitat.

WYVERN

WINGED AND WICKED

Wyverns had a snake-like body, batlike wings with sharp tips, a barbed tail, and two hind legs that allowed them to stand upright. Like Amphipteres, they were mean and ruthless creatures, attacking villages to create fear. Wyverns are considered "lesser dragons," or dragonlike creatures because they had only two legs and usually could not breathe fire.

There is a species of Wyvern known as the Sea-Wyvern, which had a fish's body, lurked in the depths of the oceans, and attacked ships.

Creature Features

Region	Europe
Time Period	Early 17th century
Habitat	Woodlands near villages
Flight Capable	Yes
Fire Breath	Sometimes

LESSER DRAGONS

The Wyvern differs from the European dragon in that it is usually depicted with two legs—and because of that, it's more like a serpent than a dragon.

SVARA

ONE DEADLY DRAGON

Lurking in Armenian folklore is this massive yellow dragon so huge that its teeth were as big as a man's arm. Svara was so deadly that people believed it could poison anything it came into contact with. That's why everyone kept their distance.

Svara's teeth were pointed at the tip and serrated—or jagged—along the sides. It had a colossal horn and large ears.

Creature Features

Region	Eastern Europe
Time Period	Unknown
Habitat	Unknown
Flight Capable	Unknown
Fire Breath	Unknown

VANQUISHED

Not much is known about Svara, except that a great hero named Keresapa was able to vanquish it.

KNUCKER

KNUCKER PIE

Knuckers were wicked water dragons. They lived in almost perfectly circular woodland waterholes fed by underground springs that kept them at a constant temperature year-round. These holes are called knuckerholes. Legend has it that one of the most wicked Knuckers was slayed by pie! Poison was baked into a dragon-size pie, which was delivered to the Knucker on a cart pulled by the horse. Of course, the Knucker ate the pie—along with the horse, and the cart—before the poison did its work.

Creature Features

Region	Britain
Time Period	8th—11th centuries
Habitat	Knuckerholes
Flight Capable	No
Fire Breath	No

TO FLY, OR NOT TO FLY

Knuckers did not fly—they preferred to lurk in dark, wet places—but they did have very small wings, which suggest that they may have flown at one time.

ZILANT

KING OF THE SERPENTS

Legend has it that people in a small Russian village lived near a pit writhing with big, venomous snakes. One day, they decided to take care of the snakes by setting the snake pit on fire and Zilant rose from the ashes. The king of the serpents, this dragon stood for wisdom and became the symbol of the Russian city of Kazan.

Creature Features

Region	Russia
Time Period	13th—16th century
Habitat	Hillsides
Flight Capable	Yes
Fire Breath	Unknown

SNEAKY SNAKES

Some legends say that Zilant wasn't one being but was instead made up of hundreds of snakes linked together in the shape of a dragon.

DRAGONS IN OTHER CULTURES

While the European dragon and those like it might be the most popular types of dragons in the Western hemisphere, dragons exist all over the world—and what you'll learn about some of them might surprise you! Aside from the European dragon, the most popular and well-known dragon in the world might just be Long, but there are other fascinating dragons with amazing abilities. Let's explore a few of them.

CHINESE DRAGON

LONG

LUCKY STARS

Here's one dragon you'd be happy to see! Long, also known as Lung or the Chinese dragon, was a kind and giving creature. Instead of bringing death and destruction, Long brought good luck and heavenly bounty. There were different types of Long; some ruled the earth, and some ruled the sea and skies.

Creature Features

Region	China
Time Period	30th century BC
Habitat	Waterways, such as rivers and lakes
Flight Capable	Yes
Fire Breath	Yes

PEARLS OF WISDOM

Long's mouth was filled with sharp, thick, and curved teeth—and also a pearl, which symbolized wisdom.

IMUGI

BECOMING DRAGONS

Imugis looked like huge pythons, with large front fangs and a forked tongue. They lived in dark and wet places. Despite their creepy appearance, they were thought to be kind and to deliver good luck. Imugis are known to help people, even if it meant harm to themselves. In one story, an Imugi defied the gods and brought rain to some much-needed crops.

Creature Features

Region	Asia
Time Period	Unknown
Habitat	Rivers, lakes, and oceans
Flight Capable	No
Fire Breath	No

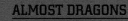

ALMOST DRAGONS

Some people believe Imugi were "protodragons," meaning creatures that would eventually become dragons, if they survived for 1,000 years, and their sighting was associated with good luck.

NĀGA

MYSTERIOUS BEINGS

Stories of the Nāga exist throughout Asia, and each description is a little bit different. According to various legends, Nāgas could have anywhere from one to five heads. The five-headed kind guarded temples in Indonesia and Thailand. To scare away intruders, Nāgas needed to look tough. And they did, especially thanks to their double set of upper teeth.

In other cultures, the Nāga aren't so nice. Stories from Malaysia describe Nāgas as monstrous evil creatures that lived in the sea and terrorized fishermen.

Creature Features

Region	Southeast Asia (Indonesia, Thailand, Malaysia, the Philippines)
Time Period	Unknown
Habitat	Oceans and waterways
Flight Capable	Unknown
Fire Breath	Unknown

ANOTHER NĀGA

The Nāgas in Indian folklore are human-snake hybrids: people from the waist up and serpents from the waist down. They are magical and godlike, and beautiful and strong. Nāga-loka, the underground world where they live, is gorgeous, and their buildings are decorated with sparkling gems.

PAKHANGBA

WOODLAND WONDER

Not much is known about this unique creature, though some think that—like the Nāga—it offered protection to special places. A mix between a serpent and a deer with large antlers, Pakhangba lived near the sacred ponds and woodland groves of northeastern India. Pakhangba's deer antlers may symbolize gentleness and kindness.

Creature Features

Region	India
Time Period	Unknown
Habitat	Mountains and caves, as well as lakes
Flight Capable	Yes
Fire Breath	No

CURIOUSLY COILED

Pakhangba is often pictured coiled with its own tail in its mouth—clamped between the four curved fangs in its upper and lower jaws.

ETHIOPIAN DRAGON

DRAGONS WITH DRACONITAS

Ethiopian dragons were enormous creatures that lived in eastern Africa. They hunted elephants, so they had to have very strong, thick teeth to first grab and then rip through meaty prey. When their food source was scarce, Ethiopian dragons could wrap themselves together and float across the sea in search of more food.

According to legend, Ethiopian dragons had magical stones in their skulls called Draconitas. For the Draconitas to keep their power, they had to be taken out of dragons while the creatures were still alive. The best way to do this? Lull the dragon to sleep with special herbs first.

Creature Features

Region	Eastern Africa
Time Period	Unknown
Habitat	Dry deserts
Flight Capable	Yes
Fire Breath	Unknown

I AM GROOTSLANG

Grootslang is a monster from African myths whose name means "great snake," and this huge serpent could grow up to 60 feet (18 m). In South African lore, the gods realized they made a mistake when they created Grootslang, and split the monster into two smaller creatures: elephants and snakes.

AMARU

SPITTING RAINBOWS

A massive serpentlike creature that lived underground, Amaru also had wings and feet like a bird's—so it could crawl out from the depths and take to the sky. This two-headed creature had one head looked like a llama's. The other resembled a puma's and was filled with smooth hooked fangs.

Amaru was an important part of Incan mythology, and Incans believed that Amaru could move between the real world and the spiritual one.

Creature Features

Region	Peru
Time Period	13th century
Habitat	Underground caves
Flight Capable	Yes
Fire Breath	No

THE RAINMAKER

Incans believed Amaru could create rainbows. They thought that one of Amaru's heads would sip in water from a spring and then spit a stream into the air to land in the mouth of its other head. The water's arc was a rainbow. Amaru was also believed to bring rain and out-of-this-world events.

DRAGONLIKE CREATURES AND LEGENDARY BEASTS

In addition to dragons and lesser dragons, mythology is filled with dragonlike beasts and other mythical monsters. Here are just a few of the notable ones from around the world.

CREATURES AND BEASTS

HYDRA

HOW MANY HEADS?

Behold the Hydra! The Hydra had poisonous blood and gave off deadly fumes. And if that weren't awful enough, it also had anywhere from six or more heads—and if one were cut off, multiple heads would sprout in its place.

Creature Features

Region	Mediterranean
Time Period	8th—6th century BC
Habitat	The swamp outside Lake Lerna
Flight Capable	No
Fire Breath	No

A TRUE STAR

This beast was a star of Greek myths. Hydra was the offspring of Echidna and Typhon, who gave birth to many mythical monsters, including the Chimera. Like many dragons, Hydra loved water. It lurked in Lerna, a lake that was one entryway to the Underworld.

CHIMERA

THE MONSTER MASH

Part dragon, part lion, and part goat, the Chimera is a scary hybrid creature. Chimera was Hydra's sister, and like Hydra, she terrorized the people of ancient Greece. A hero named Bellerophon was only able to beat her with the help of Pegasus, the winged horse.

People were so fascinated by Chimera's hybrid body that the word chimera today can mean any amazing mashup of creatures or ideas.

Creature Features

Region	Southern Europe (Greece)
Time Period	8th—6th century BC
Habitat	Waterways, such as rivers and lakes
Flight Capable	Yes
Fire Breath	Unknown

CENTURIES-OLD STORIES

Ancient Greeks created detailed stories known as myths. Through these tales the ancient Greeks tried to explain how the world came to be. Because these stories were so well preserved in writing and art, these myths are stories we still tell today—and that's how we know about creatures like Hydra and Chimera.

COCKATRICE

A CHILLING CHICKEN

What happens when an old chicken's egg is cared for and then hatched by a serpent? According to legend, a Cockatrice is born. A mix of dragon, rooster, and serpent, the Cockatrice had a long list of dangerous features. This horrible hybrid had the beak of its chicken ancestors. Like a bird of prey, it had a tomial tooth—a hooked beak used for tearing flesh.

The Cockatrice was so deadly, a creature could die just by looking at it. Its mere presence could kill an orchard of fruit trees, and it could poison a lake for centuries just by drinking from it.

Creature Features

Region	North Africa
Time Period	14th century
Habitat	Deserts
Flight Capable	Yes
Fire Breath	Unknown

IN HERALDRY

The Cockatrice was used as a symbol of heraldry in England as far back as the 14th century.

TARASQUE

A MENACING MIX OF MONSTERS

Picture a dragon's head on the body of an ox, with the feet of a bear. That's the terrible Tarasque, which appears in legends from southern Europe. Though most reports of the Tarasque came from southern France, it was also known as the Tarasca in southern Spain. This wicked beast preyed on villages until it was tamed and sent away by a saint.

In some legends, the Tarasque even had a turtle shell complete with spikes, as well as a scorpion's tail. Tarasque's triangular and jagged teeth were small, but its top fangs and front claws were deadly.

Creature Features

Region	Southern Europe
Time Period	Mid-13th century or before
Habitat	Riverbanks
Flight Capable	No
Fire Breath	Unknown

MEDIEVAL MONSTERS

Lots of legends were told during medieval times, and many monsters—like the Cockatrice and Tarasque—starred in these stories. Some of the other unbelievable beasts from this time include the Manticore, which had the head of a man and the body of a lion—and a tail that could shoot spikes, The Griffin was a beautiful monster, with the head and wings of an eagle but the body of a lion. Griffins were said to lay golden eggs.

CULTURAL CREATURES

We know about dragons today thanks to how well documented they are in stories, art, and cultures worldwide. Here's where you can find dragons woven into cultures in history, and where you can find dragons today.

A COAT OF ARMS

Medieval knights identified themselves by their coat of arms. No, it's not an actual coat. It's a design that includes symbols telling anyone who sees it who you are. A dragon in a coat of arms let people know that a medieval knight was a brave and honorable defender. An Amphiptere meant fierceness.

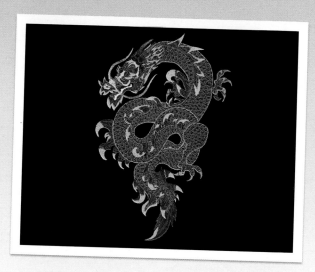

SERPENT SIGNIFIES STRENGTH

Since the dragon symbolizes wisdom and power in Asian cultures, the dragon is also the symbol for the emperor in ancient China. Imperial robes are often embroidered with scenes of dragons.

HUMAN HEALERS

Traditional Chinese medicine is the practice of using herbs and meditation to treat ailments. It began in ancient China and is still practiced today. Some people who practice Chinese medicine believe rubbing ground-up "dragon bones" on the skin over a broken bone might help it heal.

DRAGON DANCE

As you know from reading about Long, dragons are symbols of luck in Asian cultures. That's why dragons are powerful symbols for Chinese New Year, a holiday tied to the traditional Chinese calendar, which calculates years based on astrological factors. The Dragon Dance is performed on Chinese New Year. People construct a dragon out of colorful paper and fabric and then mount the creation on wood and bamboo hoops and poles. During celebrations, dancers hold the poles and move in serpentine ways, weaving and bobbing, and spreading that good dragon luck for the year to come.

DRAGON TALES

Stories inspire stories, and dragons don't exist in myths only. Movies feature sinister dragons on par with Svara and Zilant, such as Disney's *Sleeping Beauty*. Kinder dragons show up in pop culture too, in movies like *How to Train Your Dragon* and *Mulan*. Dragons appear in books too, including the Lord of the Rings series and the Harry Potter series.

We know that dragons exist in stories and culture. But is there any evidence that they walked the earth? Here are some real possibilities . . .

Pteranodon

Tyrannosaurus Rex

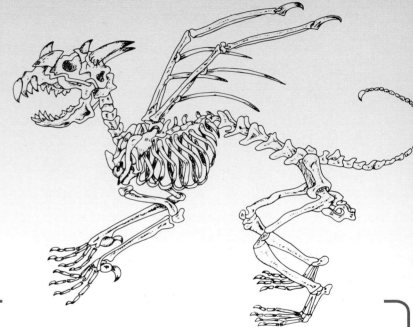

DRAGON BONES

People have known about dinosaurs—or at least their huge fossils—since about the fourth century BC. People may have created stories to try to explain huge fossil skeletons—and the idea of dragons may have been born. It's possible that a Pteranodon's skeleton could have been the inspiration for a winged monster, or a *T. rex* fossil was confused for a dragon's that lived during the Pleistocene era, about 350,000 years ago.

ARCHAEOLOGY AND THE BEAST

Dragons may not be the only mythical creature inspired by dinosaurs. Ancient people in many cultures told stories in great detail of the Griffin, an eagle-lion hybrid that laid golden eggs. An American scholar named Adrienne Mayor was interested in trying to find the source of the Griffin tales, and she thought the key might be in those golden eggs.

She searched through ancient texts, reading stories of Griffins from ancient nomads who mined for gold. Mayor then searched for a real place—a site where these nomads might have found their gold. Thanks to ancient texts, she eventually found a site in the Gobi Desert, in Asia, rich with mineral deposits. But the area was rich in something else, too: dinosaur fossils, and fossils of one dinosaur in particular.

Protoceratops was an early Cretaceous period relative of the Triceratops. It had a beak and claws, large leg bones, and strong shoulder bones that might have looked like wings. And ancient travelers may have found Protoceratops's skeleton jutting through the desert floor thanks to erosion. From this, Mayor hypothesized, the story of the Griffin might have been created.

RHINO-DRAGON!

The town of Klagenfurt, Austria, was said to have been tormented for years by a giant Lindworm. Thankfully, heroic knights saved the day by slaying the horrible monster. For years, Klagenfurt's town hall displayed that dragon's skull. Or so they thought. Later analysis showed that the skull actually belonged to a wooly rhinoceros, a huge and hairy prehistoric mammal that lived more than 11,700 years ago.

Protoceratops

It's not just long-extinct dinosaurs that could have inspired dragon tales. Here are some actual animals that might be the creatures behind mythical creations . . .

LARGE REPTILES

Reptiles like the Nile Crocodile or monitor lizards could account for some dragon stories. Crocodiles lurk in riverbanks and stay mostly hidden underwater while hunting, exposing just their eyes and snout, leaving the rest of their body up to the imagination.

HUGE SNAKES

Serpents figure so heavily in what dragons look like, it's possible that tales of huge snakes similar to today's anacondas or reticulated pythons could account for dragon tales.

WHALES

These truly giant creatures have inspired countless tales among fishermen. But washed ashore, their bones could resemble that of a giant dragonlike beast.

MODERN DRAGONS

They may not breathe fire, but dragons exist in the world today—or at least animals that have been named after dragons and other mythical beasts. Here are some of the fierce and fascinating creatures that are our modern-day dragons, and why they get to carry the legendary name.

DRAGONSNAKE

Almost as rare as dragons themselves, dragonsnakes are hard-to-find serpents that live in the forests of Indonesia, Malaysia, and sometimes Thailand and Burma. They can grow up to 2.5 feet (0.8 m), and they feed mostly on frogs.

Scientific Name: *Xenodermus javanicus*

Other names	Javan mudsnake	Flight Capable	No
Region	Southeast Asia	Fire Breath	No
Habitat	Rainforests		

WHAT MAKES THEM DRAGONLIKE?

Most snakes have scales that lie flat, giving them a smooth feel. But dragonsnakes are known for the ridges of rough scales that run down their back, giving them a fierce, scaly, dragonlike appearance. These ridges also give dragonsnakes their scientific name, *Xenodermus*. It means "strange skin."

DRAGONFLY

With about 3,000 species buzzing around the world, dragonflies range in sizes and colors. But they all have huge, sharp-sighted eyes and two pairs of large veined wings. Dragonflies are ancient creatures, and their existence on earth dates back 300 million years—even before the dinosaurs. Though today the largest of these insects have wingspans of about 6 inches (15 cm), fossils of dragonflies have wingspans measuring 2 feet (0.6 m).

Scientific Name: *Anisoptera (suborder)*

Other names	Darner, Devil's Arrow	Flight Capable	Yes
Region	Worldwide, except in polar regions	Fire Breath	No
Habitat	Near freshwater		

DRAGONFISH

Dragonfish are small—they grow to only about 6.5 inches (16.5 cm). But they make up for their small size with their big mouth filled with huge fangs. These deep-sea fish lure in prey with special bioluminescent photophores, which are organs that glow in the dark. The light brings curious fish close, and then the dragonfish use their needlelike teeth to snatch them up.

Scientific Name: *Stomiidae (family)*

Other names	Seamouth	Flight Capable	No
Region	Indo-Pacific waters	Fire Breath	No
Habitat	Deep sea		

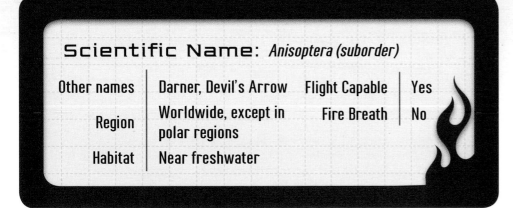

Like dragons, dragonflies are excellent predators and speedy hunters. They are able to attack and eat other insects in midair. But according to some stories, dragonflies got their name from the legend of St. George. St. George fought and slayed a dragon that had poisoned and terrorized a town. To fight back—or so the story goes—the devil turned St. George's horse into a flying bug, named the dragonfly.

What makes them dragonlike?

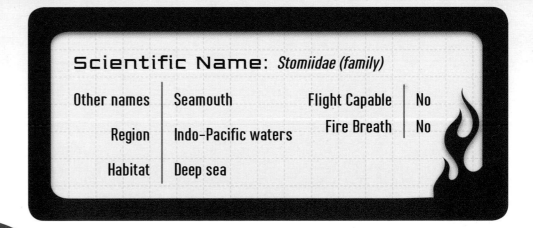

Huge fangs aren't the only characteristics that dragonfish share with dragons. They also have a long body that tapers to a tail-like fin. Their large bony pectoral, or side, fins fan out like underwater wings.

DRAGON MILLIPEDE

Dragon millipedes lurk in dark, damp places, like the deepest corners of caves. They're small—about 1 inch (3 cm) long—but deadly. Dragon millipedes give off cyanide, which is a poison. Aside from their tough look, all species of dragon millipedes are brightly colored, like the shocking pink dragon millipede. Their bright colors are a warning to would-be predators that taking a bite would be a bad idea.

Scientific Name: *Desmoxytes purpurosea*

Other names	Unknown	Flight Capable	No
Region	Southeast Asia	Fire Breath	No
Habitat	Caves		

WHAT MAKES THEM DRAGONLIKE?

Dragon millipedes have spikes that run the length of their body. This tough-looking armor probably protects their many legs. Between their spikes and their poison, dragon millipedes earn their dragon title.

BEARDED DRAGON

You might recognize these popular pets. Bearded dragons are easygoing reptiles who do well in captivity. In the wild, they sun themselves in deserts and feed on leaves, fruits, and sometimes insects and other lizards. When a bearded dragon meets another bearded dragon, they wave at each other. It's a way to tell their fellow dragons from other lizard species.

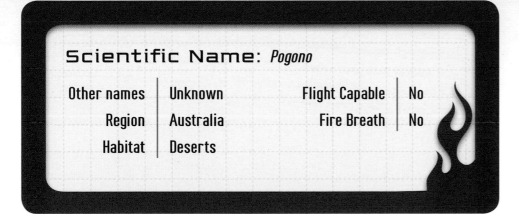

Scientific Name: *Pogono*

Other names	Unknown	Flight Capable	No
Region	Australia	Fire Breath	No
Habitat	Deserts		

DRACO LIZARD

A draco lizard on a tree branch may not look very exciting. They're small and brown, and feed on small insects and termites. But these little lizards have a big surprise. They have special flaps of skin along their sides that they can expand, like wings. All it takes is a running jump from a tree branch and opening those flaps, and these lizards are airborne.

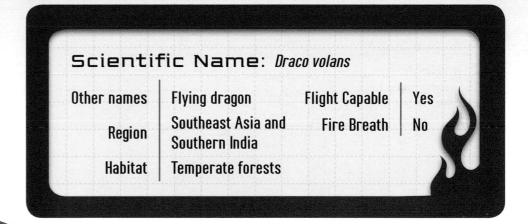

Scientific Name: *Draco volans*

Other names	Flying dragon	Flight Capable	Yes
Region	Southeast Asia and Southern India	Fire Breath	No
Habitat	Temperate forests		

Like other reptiles we've covered in this book, bearded dragons have a dragon resemblance. But they're better known for their beard, the little spiky barbs under their chin. If they're threatened by a possible predator, bearded dragons puff out their throats, making the beard grow—and making the lizard look larger.

What makes them dragonlike?

At 8 inches (20 cm), these flying reptiles are like mini dragons. But they don't really fly. Their wings of skin don't flap like a bird's wings. Instead, they take huge leaps, which can help them travel more than 20 feet (6 m) through the air, allowing them to leap from tree to tree.

KOMODO DRAGON

These 10-foot-long (3-m-long) giant lizards are the largest lizards in the world. They're top predators built for hunting: They have razor-sharp teeth, claws made for ripping, keen tracking senses, and powerful muscles.

Scientific Name: *Varanus komodoensis*

Other names	Komodo monitor	Flight Capable	No
Region	Indonesia	Fire Breath	No
Habitat	Tropical forests and beaches		

WHAT MAKES THEM DRAGONLIKE?

Komodo dragons have serpentlike bodies, four legs equipped with powerful claws, and deadly bites. They're just missing flight and fire breath to be perfect modern-day dragons.

FRILLED DRAGON

Frilled dragons hang out on tree trunks and branches, where they can camouflage themselves against the bark and hide out from predators. Sometimes, they hunt for prey on the ground. Away from the trees, the frilled dragon can be exposed to predators. But they're not totally defenseless. If they feel threatened, these dragons stand up, open their mouths, and show their frills—flaps of skin that unfurl to make the lizard look much bigger and scarier than they are. Some dragons have frills that measure up to a foot wide.

LEAFY SEADRAGONS

Colorful and wildly camouflaged, leafy seadragons blend in with seaweed and float with the tides. They're not the best swimmers, but that's okay—they don't really need to go anywhere, as they suck in nutrients from seawater.

Scientific Name: *Phycodurus eques*

Other names	Unknown	Flight Capable	No
Region	Southern Australia	Fire Breath	No
Habitat	Seaweed beds in shallow waters		

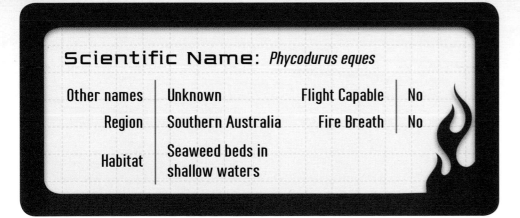

Scientific Name: *Chlamydosaurus kingii*

Other names	Frill-necked lizard	Flight Capable	No
Region	Northern Australia, New Guinea	Fire Breath	No
Habitat	Woodlands		

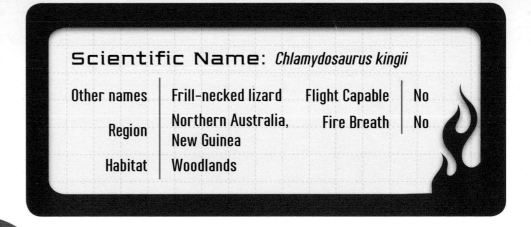

Seadragons have dragonlike faces. But that's about all these gentle, delicate creatures have in common with their fierce namesakes.

What makes them dragonlike?

Their reptilian looks and seemingly fierce demeanor earn this frilled lizard its dragon name. But despite their appearance, frilled dragons are really peaceful creatures.

GLOSSARY

Airborne
Being off the ground and carried through the air

Bounty
A reward, or an abundance of something that has been given generously

Carnivore
Animal that eats other animals

Century
A period of 100 years

Characteristic
A unique trait or quality of something

Coat of Arms
A special symbolic emblem to identify a family, town, or organization

Colossal
Having gigantic size and proportions

Cretaceous Period
The last period of the Mesozoic era characterized by the dominance of reptiles

Earthquake
A shaking or trembling of the Earth, perhaps volcanic or tectonic in origin

Era
A very long unit of time divided into shorter units called periods

Extinct
No longer existing

Features
The characteristics that make up something's appearance

Flammable
Capable of being easily ignited and burning quickly

Folklore
Stories, tales, or sayings that have been preserved and passed down from generation to generation among a people group

Fossil
Preserved body parts of traces of an animal or plant

Gargoyle
A spout in the form of an ugly human or animal figure projecting from a roof gutter to disperse rainwater

Habitat
A place where a plant or animal lives naturally

Hybrid
An offspring of two animals of different species

Lance
A steel-tipped spear or sharp object carri by a knight

Landscape
The natural features of land in a particular region

Legend
An inspiring story passed down from generation to generation

Livestock
Animals raised or kept, usually for farm us

Lore
A body of knowledge or tradition that is learned from a previous generation

edieval
tiquated, or characterized by the Middle
es

iddle Ages
e period of history from about a.d. 500 to
out 1500

yth
popular belief or traditional story of
storical events that serve to describe a
tural occurrence

arl
smooth, rounded bead formed within the
ells of mollusks, often used as jewelry and
sociated with wealth

egasus
winged horse in Greek mythology

eriod
unit of time millions of years long

eistocene
geological time often referred to as the Ice
ge

Predator
An animal that hunts and kills other animals
for food

Prehistoric
Existing before written history

Prey
An animal that is hunted and eaten by
predators

Pteranodon
Any animal from the genus of extinct flying
reptiles having a backwardly directed bony
crest on the skull and a wingspan of about
25 feet

Region
A broad geographic area of the world

Reticulated
Resembling a net, or a network

Sacrifice
An offering made to a deity or someone in
power

Serpent
A snakelike creature

Serrated
Notched or toothed on the edge

Slay
To kill or strike down

Sulfur
A pale-yellow element that occurs in nature,
such as volcanic deposits and natural gas,
and is used to make gunpowder for its
flammable quality

Triceratops
A type of dinosaur with three horns and a
parrotlike beak

Vanquish
To overcome in battle

Venomous
Full of poison

Victor
One who defeats an enemy or opponent

Waterspouts
A pipe or duct that carries and spouts water

Wisdom
Good sense and judgment

Woodlands
Land covered with woody vegetation

Quarto Knows

Inspiring | Educating | Creating | Entertaining

Brimming with creative inspiration, how-to projects, and useful information to enrich your everyday life, Quarto Knows is a favorite destination for those pursuing their interests and passions. Visit our site and dig deeper with our books into your area of interest: Quarto Creates, Quarto Cooks, Quarto Homes, Quarto Lives, Quarto Drives, Quarto Explores, Quarto Gifts, or Quarto Kids.

© 2019 Quarto Publishing Group USA Inc.
Text © 2019

Produced in 2019 by becker&mayer!, an imprint of The Quarto Group, 11120 NE 33rd Place, Suite 201, Bellevue, WA 98004 USA.
www.QuartoKnows.com

All rights reserved. No part of this book may be reproduced in any form without written permission of the copyright owners. All images in this book have been reproduced with the knowledge and prior consent of the artists concerned, and no responsibility is accepted by producer, publisher, or printer for any infringement of copyright or otherwise, arising from the contents of this publication. Every effort has been made to ensure that credits accurately comply with information supplied. We apologize for any inaccuracies that may have occurred and will resolve inaccurate or missing information in a subsequent reprinting of the book.

19 20 21 22 23   5 4 3 2 1

ISBN: 978-0-7603-6585-4

Library of Congress Cataloging-in-Publication Data is available.

Author: L. J. Tracosas
Illustrator: RJ Palmer & Kerem Beyit
Design: Kate Sinclair
Editorial: Bonnie Honeycutt
Production: Yuhong Guo
Product Development: Todd Rider
Modeling: Nelson Turek

Printed, manufactured, and assembled in Shenzhen, China, 05/19

MIX
Paper from responsible sources
FSC® C017606

Image credits (images used throughout):
Vector mountains and treetops, and jungle illustration © SaveJungle/Shutterstock; Vector dragon and griffin silhouettes © Darkness222/Shutterstock; Vector flame © sabbracadabra/Shutterstock; 3D dragon skeleton rendering © Nelson Turek; Vector dragon head silhouette © EVKA/Shutterstock; 3D blue and gray dragon renderings and 3D gray wings rendering © Valentyna Chukhlyebova/Shutterstock; 3D red dragon rendering © DM7/Shutterstock; Blue fog © iKatod/Shutterstock; Earth © ixpert/Shutterstock; Ancient world map © Harbar Liudmyla/Shutterstock; Gold dragon statue © seaskylab/Shutterstock; Gold dragon © Tonis Pan/Shutterstock; Dragon skull © Victor Moussa/Shutterstock; Dragon egg © WICHAI WONGJONGJAIHAN/Shutterstock; 3D dragon tail rendering © tsuneomp/Shutterstock; 3D blue and green dragon renderings © Warpaint/Shutterstock; Red dragon scales © bokehboutique/Shutterstock; Flames © Lukas Gojda/Shutterstock; Red dragon face © Refluo/Shutterstock; Green dragon eye © Gorelova Evgeniya/Shutterstock; Dragon body © Andreas Meyer/Shutterstock; Row of flames © Potapov Alexander/Shutterstock; Bat and bird wing © Aldona Griskeviciene/Shutterstock; Flying bat © Rudmer Zwerver/Shutterstock; Flying bird © Victor Tyakht/Shutterstock; Rocky mountaintop © chaiyapruek youprasert/Shutterstock; Dragon bearing teeth © Laslo Ludrovan/Shutterstock; Medieval knight © Algol/Shutterstock; Painting of St. George © Everett - Art/Shutterstock; Knight with sword and shield © FXQuadro/Shutterstock; Vector gargoyle on pedestal and bird talon © draco77vector/Shutterstock; Vector dragon open mouth © Zsschreiner/Shutterstock; Vector sheep © Forest Foxy/Shutterstock; Vector flag of wales © oxameel/Shutterstock; Vector hand with sword © NatBasil/Shutterstock; Vector top of flying dragon © Shyshell/Shutterstock; Vector snake silhouette © archivector/Shutterstock; Vector dragon sharp teeth © vectortwins/Shutterstock; Vector four leaf clover © Oakview Studios/Shutterstock; Vector snake with mouth open © TRONIN ANDREI/Shutterstock; Vector dragon eating tail © sahua d/Shutterstock; Vector elephant silhouette © Robert Adrian Hillman/Shutterstock; Vector open book © bioraven/Shutterstock; Vector dragon sitting profile © Shyshell/Shutterstock; Vector shield with axes © GoMixer/Shutterstock; Vector griffin © PO11/Shutterstock; Vector knight on horse with flag © rudall30/Shutterstock; Chinese medicine © Dragon Images/Shutterstock; Vector herb illustrations © Foxyliam/Shutterstock; Colorful dragon embroidery © Lavrushka/Shutterstock; Dragon reading book illustration © Sacramento Bee/Contributor/Getty Images; Chinese dragon costume © 1000nokotoba/Shutterstock; People holding chinese dragon © crazybike/Shutterstock; Vector Chinese lanterns © artskvortsova/Shutterstock; Pteranodon fossil © AKKHARAT JARUSILAWONG/Shutterstock; Tyrannosaurus rex fossil © Ton Bangkeaw/Shutterstock; Vector dragon skeleton illustration © Vera Petruk/Shutterstock; Wooly rhinoceros rendering © Daniel Eskridge/Shutterstock; Protoceratops skeleton © breckeni/Getty Images; Griffin illustration © PARFENOV1976/Shutterstock; Golden eggs © Mike_O/Shutterstock; Photo corners © Nevada31/Shutterstock; Vector crocodile illustration © mamita/Shutterstock; Vector grass illustration © Vertyr/Shutterstock; Vector python illustration © matyas/Shutterstock; Vector whale illustration © intueri/Shutterstock; Vector undersea illustration © Nechayka/Shutterstock; Whale skeleton on beach © Mark Anthony Ray/Shutterstock; Dragonsnake © reptiles4all/Shutterstock; Dragonfly © AMNAT DPP/Shutterstock; Scaly Dragonfish drawing by G. Brown Goode and Tarleton H. Bean, published 1896, courtesy of public domain; Dragon millipede © Jarun Tedjaem/Shutterstock; Bearded dragon © Elina Litovkina/Shutterstock; Draco lizard © NaniP/Shutterstock; Komodo dragon © Anna Kucherova/Shutterstock; Frilled dragon © Ais Qocak/Shutterstock; Leafy seadragon © Kjersti Joergensen/Shutterstock

324168

ASSEMBLING THE SKELETON

1. Start with the dragon skull. Attach the bottom jaw. Then insert the post of vertebrae 1 into the back of the skull.
2. Attach the ribcage sides together into vertebrae 1.
3. Piece rear legs together and then attach to vertebrae 1.
4. Attach right foreleg to right scapula.
5. Attach left and right scapulas to left and right ribcages.
6. Piece tail sections together (vertebrae 2 and 3), then attach to rear of vertebrae 1.
7. Attach wings. Note: Thumbs point down to determine left and right wing.

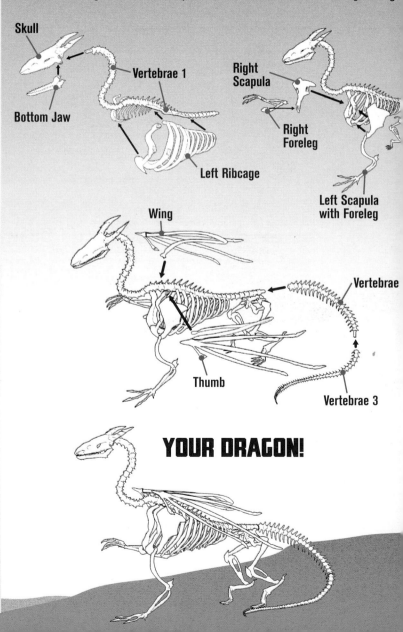

YOUR DRAGON!